Historical Things it Shouldn't Have and Why the Heck They Happened

25 More Funny Stories of Weird History of the World and Fun Facts Everyone Should Know Just Because
Volume 2

PABLO VANNUCCI

Copyright © 2023 Pablo Vannucci

All rights reserved.

ISBN: 9798871558829

DEDICATION

For all those people who would stop
what they're doing to go outside
to witness a wandering hippo,
I hope you enjoy wandering through
these weird things in history.

CONTENTS

	Introduction	1
1	The Great Emu War	5
2	Mustache Cups	9
3	Phone Booth Stuffing	12
4	The Really Nice Interrogator	15
5	Dance 'til You Drop	19
6	Rest in Pizza	22
7	The Ribbiting Battery	25
8	Honey, I'm Smothered	28
9	The Wild Wild Camels	31
10	Alexander the Buried	34
11	Smart Dunce Caps	37
12	The Man Who Ate Everything	40
13	The Sticky Tsunami	44
14	Turkey Worship	47
15	Dog Lover Extreme	50
16	The War on Cats	53
17	Huberta the Hippo	56
18	Electrifying Fashions	59
19	The Moldy Bread Cure	62
20	The Taj Bamboo	65
21	Orchidelirium	68

22	To Grandma's House By Mail	71
23	The French Town That Went Mad	74
24	Halley's Gases	77
25	Tomato on Trial	81
	Afterward	85
	About the Author	89

PRAISE FOR *WEIRD THINGS IN HISTORY*

"Understanding history is of utmost significance, as it imparts valuable knowledge and enlightens us about pivotal occurrences that transpired in the past. Due to the aspects of the book I enjoyed, I rate it 5 out of 5 stars and recommend it to readers seeking a non-fictional book of historical events from the past." - **Davy Ifedigbo, OnlineBookClub.org**

"You have collected a fun and often bizarre array of historical anecdotes suitable for reading a little bit every day or breeze through in one sitting. Your tongue in cheek approach is sure to delight readers. The stories The Glass Delusion and The Novl with No 'E' are especially daffy." - **Judge, 32nd Annual Writer's Digest Self-Published Book Awards**

"This book strikes the perfect balance between education and entertainment. The author presents the facts, skillfully narrating each bizarre tale, while ensuring that the reader remains thoroughly engaged and entertained. Its perfect blend of facts, storytelling, and entertaining sketches make it an absolute must-read for history enthusiasts, curious minds, and anyone seeking an unforgettable journey through the stranger side of our past." - **Bonnie V., Amazon Reviewer**

"*Weird History* is a delightful anthology of amusing stories that follows a clever three-part structure: the facts, the story, and the breakdown. The stories are expertly crafted to tickle the reader's funny bone, leaving a lasting smile in their wake. As a quick and enjoyable read, *Weird History* offers a refreshing blend of humor and insight, making it a must-read for anyone seeking laughter and enlightenment." - **Joseph V., Amazon Reviewer**

PRAISE FOR *WEIRD THINGS IN HISTORY*

"Sometimes, all I want is to escape from reality and indulge in some mindless reading. This book fits the bill perfectly. It's impossible not to smile while reading it. Moreover, the book's structure is fantastic. It grabs your attention like a skilled reporter. Overall, it's an incredibly enjoyable read." **- Leila A., Amazon Reviewer**

"The author's lighthearted and witty narrative style makes history come alive with a fresh and engaging twist. Each story is a blend of entertainment and education, offering a glimpse into moments that might not find their way into traditional history textbooks." **- Tricia C., Amazon Reviewer**

"I knew some of these stories, but it was cool to hear the back story. If you like reading about weird, true stories, then you will love this book." **- Mark G., Amazon Reviewer**

"I loved every page of this book! It is thought-provoking, funny, and informative without being dull! I definitely recommend it to anyone that loves history, weird facts, or both!" **- Jenny L., Amazon Reviewer**

"Fact is definitely stranger than fiction as this entertaining book proves. Pablo Vannucci's engaging narration of the weird and wonderful makes this book a real page turner. It contains over 25 bizarre historical tales, each one more unbelievable than the previous. This book turns the often ho-humness of history books on its head so that it will delight historians and non-historians alike. Fascinating!" **- Joanne K., Amazon Reviewer**

DOWNLOAD YOUR VISUAL COMPANION!

Unlock the strangest moments in history with the digital timeline companion to *Weird Things in History and Why the Heck They Happened Volume 2*. As you read, this visual guide lets you trace the timeline of odd events, bringing the book's bizarre stories to life.

Featuring vibrant illustrations, this graphic makes history fun and memorable. Whether you're reading along with the book or diving into the timeline solo, this digital download is a must-have for any history enthusiast.

Enhance your reading journey, share it with friends, or use it as a unique teaching tool. With this timeline, you'll never see history the same way again!

Download Now!
https://pablovannucci.com/weird-things-in-history

INTRODUCTION

Weird Things in History and Why the Heck They Happened returns in its second volume! Like *Volume 1*, this book is about exploring some of the funniest and just plain craziest historical events you may or may not have heard of. Because you're reading this book, we hope you enjoyed *Volume 1*, where we dove into some peculiar events such as the glass delusion of the Middle Ages, the luxurious obsession of the pineapple in 18th-century England, and the fruity apple-tossing sign of love in ancient Greece. We promise this second installment will be just as fun, insightful, and downright weird.

In the archives of history, an endless number of odd events defy explanation, leaving us with a little bit of bewilderment and astonishment. From unexplainable phenomena to bizarre incidents, these strange happenings have fascinated and perplexed the world for generations. You most likely won't find them lying around in a school textbook or on any list when you do a basic "what are some historical events" search online. That's too bad. If the weird facts popped up first, history would be a lot more fun to study.

Each weird event in this book, or each chapter, comes in three parts. Part 1, called "The Fact," explains the weird historical event. Part 2 is called "The Story," where we'll take a deep dive into the specific circumstances surrounding the event, the historical setting, the people involved, and why it has the honor of popping up in a book dedicated to all things weird history. Part 3 is called "The Breakdown," where we'll fast forward to the present and look at the impact the historical event may have on our world today and any lessons we can learn from it.

Are you ready for your next weird history lesson? You'll meet some of the not-as-popular historical figures like a German interrogator who was just a really nice guy, some ancient Egyptians whose job it was to walk around with coats of honey dripping off of them, a wandering hippo who might have been searching for a long-lost love, and a barber who was convinced the tomato was pure evil. We promise to take you on an informative, entertaining, and perhaps unsettling journey with these additional 25 historical events. Because sometimes, the weirder things in history are the ones that teach us the most about ourselves and our world.

CHAPTER 1:
THE GREAT EMU WAR

Part 1: The Fact

An epic conflict raged in the farmlands of Australia in 1932. The wispy stalks of wheat didn't stand a chance as this blockbuster battle carried on around them. It wasn't a conflict between nations, people, or even kangaroos.

Instead, it was a conflict between humankind and a powerful flightless bird called the emu. This was the Great Emu War, an odd and humorous incident that actually resulted in a rather feathery victory.

Part 2: The Story

The Campion district of Western Australia is where it all began. The farmers, minding their own business and doing farmer-related activities like farming, kept catching glimpses of these floating heads out in the middle of their wheat fields. They quickly discovered these floating heads weren't aliens drawing crop circles but emus. There were a lot of them, and they were hungry.

The numerous emus ate through the Campion farmers' crops so quickly that they caused the locals to grow increasingly concerned about their livelihoods. These giant, flightless birds stomped over the wheat fields like feathered tanks, consuming everything in their path.

The emus typically lived near the coast, but it was that time of year when they migrated inland to breed and find food. An estimated 20,000 emus must have been pleasantly surprised to find their annual vacation spot a newly developed farmland with plenty of wheat laid out for them like a scrumptious picnic.

The wheat crops didn't stand a chance from the sudden invasion. It was understandable why the farmers were upset, especially given that they already had trouble with their crops because of the Great Depression. They couldn't have been too thrilled to see their hard work being devoured by these seemingly unstoppable two-legged birds.

In an attempt to rid their farmland of the avian invasion, the farmers contacted the Australian government for help. It was entirely acceptable in 1932 to take action against these birds. Up until 1922, the birds had been protected as a native species, but they were now considered to be vermin.

The government swiftly responded by dispatching a small army with machine guns. Many of the farmers were ex-soldiers, so they demanded machine guns as well. The fact that the government's initial reaction to the message "Please help us remove these birds from our land" was to bring in machine guns seems a little drastic and unnecessary. There must not have been any oversized cats around to chase them out.

The machine guns proved to be unnecessary and pointless in the long run. The soldiers marched into war against the emus with guns and strong aspirations. They first approached a group of 50 emus and tried to herd them together to ambush them. They had no idea, though, that these birds weren't like ostriches about to stick their heads in the ground in defeat.

Due to their speed and cleverness, the emus outwitted the soldiers at every turn- literally. Their long legs carried them far from danger as they twisted and turned, dodging everyone and everything. Emus can run as fast as 31 miles an hour. Every group of birds the soldiers came across dashed away in a feathered frenzy. The emus proved to be cunning foes, mocking the soldiers with each swift step.

The soldiers eventually realized that the emus' agility was more than a match for their machine guns. Many of the bullets that fell to the ground missed their feathered targets. Undeterred, the emus carried on their field-raiding rampage. The soldiers were left wondering how a battle with birds could turn into such a farce.

As the days went on, the Australian government saw that their feathered adversaries were winning the conflict. They must have felt pretty foolish. They ended up calling off the operation after admitting defeat to the relentless emus.

The birds went back to living in the wild, leaving the farmers to pick up the pieces of their destroyed crops. It's safe to say that the emus emerged victorious from this peculiar conflict.

Part 3: The Breakdown

The Great Emu War reminds us that even the best-laid plans can sometimes go wrong. It serves as a lesson of the value of carefully planning and taking into account every single detail before beginning any project. It also emphasizes the necessity of innovative problem-solving and flexibility when confronted with unforeseen difficulties.

In today's world, we frequently find ourselves in challenging and uncontrollable circumstances. We might face issues that seem impossible, much like the emu invasion. But keep in mind that we can all learn from our failures, just as the troops did from their defeat. Think about the Great Emu War the next time you find yourself facing a flock of emus (metaphorically speaking, of course). Adopt a creative mindset, maintain a positive outlook, and never forget that sometimes, the most unlikely solutions can bring about success.

CHAPTER 2: MUSTACHE CUPS

Part 1: The Fact

In the stylish Victorian era of the late 1860s, those with magnificent mustaches had a problem that baffled even the most prim and proper tea drinker. Enjoying a cup of simmering hot tea while sporting a beautifully maintained mustache was just simply impossible.

Like a daring deep-sea diver, the mustache had the nerve to dip into the warm teacup, leaving the unfortunate mustachioed man in a sticky, unattractive situation. Oh, the unspeakable troubles the Victorians had to face. Enter the miraculous mustache cup, a solution to this hairy problem.

Part 2: The Story

The mustache cup was created with the intention of protecting the mustache from an unplanned tea bath. Men in the Victorian era loved their mustaches, maybe a little too much. It was a peak time for facial hair etiquette, involving meticulous manuals and grooming products like whisker dye and the pocket-sized mustache comb. Hot tea could be dangerous for a mustache that had been extensively waxed since the tea could melt it and send its corners tumbling from their original proud position. Not to mention, any wax dripping into the tea itself probably wasn't too tasty or healthy.

The design of these cups was simple yet efficient. With a tiny hole for the tea to flow through, a small, semicircular guard or ledge protruded from the lip of the cup over the tea, serving as a barrier between the beverage and the mustache. Basically, it was a sippy cup. The mustache would sit on the ledge above the cup but would never have to touch the piping hot tea.

In addition to their practical function, these mustache cups frequently featured decorative elements that gave an otherwise ordinary item a whimsical touch. Delicate patterns, vibrant motifs, or even the person's initials, were worked into the porcelain. These cups almost seemed to say, "Don't worry, your mustache shall remain unscathed, and your tea-drinking experience shall be as delightful as your facial hair."

The mustache cup craze peaked in popularity in the late 19th century when it seemed like every distinguished gentleman sported mustaches. The mustache's appeal started to decline during the next few decades, though, and with it, the need for mustache cups.

Part 3: The Breakdown

Now that we know about these old-time mustache cups, we can't help but see some similarities between this strange historical event and our current environment. Today, we also use a variety of precautions to protect our prized identities and individualities. To protect ourselves from the occasionally choppy sea of public scrutiny, we build our own metaphorical mustache cups, from privacy settings on social media to personal limits.

The mustache cups also act as a reminder that even the most commonplace items may represent individuality. We can be inspired by the mustache cup's ability to blur the gap between functionality and beauty in today's environment.

CHAPTER 3:
PHONE BOOTH STUFFING

Part 1: The Fact

With the debut of what some people thought would be a short-lived trend in the form of a little box called television emerged another actual short-lived trend called phone booth stuffing.

It's exactly what it sounds like. The unusual phenomenon of phone booth stuffing swept the world in the late 1950s, where groups of people would cram as many of themselves as possible into a phone booth just to see how many would fit. Well, if you have nothing else to do, go for it.

Part 2: The Story

The beginnings of phone booth stuffing can be traced back to South Africa in 1959 when 25 college students jammed themselves into a phone booth just to see if they could. They submitted a photo of themselves to the Guinness Book of World Records, and that was when the strange new trend took over the world. Just picture a phone booth filled to the brim with arms, legs, and heads protruding in all directions like a clown car gone crazy, faces pressed against the glass in a chaotic ballet of silliness. People from all walks of life were captivated by this bizarre act, which spread like wildfire across the world and captured imaginations. Everyone was ready to try to shatter the record and delight in the sheer silliness of it all.

There weren't really any set rules on how to fit as many people inside a phone booth as possible. Some only required more than half of a person's body to be inside the booth to count, while others allowed their arms and legs to poke out.

In England, where the act was known as "telephone booth squash," someone had to be able to make a successful phone call once the booth was completely filled. Elsewhere, some even pushed the phone booths onto their side and piled in as if it were a canoe. Others attempted to use their geometry studies by using calculations to optimize angles and space. Too bad the first handheld calculator wouldn't be invented for another eight years. That would have come in handy.

Phone booth stuffing was particularly captivating because it transcended cultures and borders. It spread like a phone call to nations like the United States, Canada, Australia, and other places, becoming a worldwide phenomenon. People from all walks of life came together to experience the silly thrill of packing themselves into phone booths.

The trend quickly fizzled out within a year, however. But that was only because people found something else to stuff themselves into, like Volkswagen Beetles. This was known as "car stuffing."

Part 3: The Breakdown

People were able to literally think outside the box and discover delight in the most unexpected places because of this crazy trend. Phone booth stuffing demonstrates the limitless inventiveness and creativity that we have. It's a timely reminder to embrace our inner child and look for joy in the little things in a world that frequently feels burdened by obligations and worry.

Phone booth stuffing seems to be a charming relic from a bygone era to us today in an age dominated by technology and virtual interactions with rarely any phone booth in sight. However, it makes us stop and think about how important actual human interactions and experiences are. While screens and virtual connections may be a large part of our lives now, there is unquestionably something wonderful about physically sharing a moment of joy and fun with those around us.

In the end, phone booth stuffing may have only been a passing trend, but its spirit lives on, reminding us that sometimes the most memorable experiences in life are the ones that make us chuckle, roll our eyes, and wonder, "What on earth were we thinking?"

CHAPTER 4:
THE REALLY NICE INTERROGATOR

Part 1: The Fact

In the chaotic time of World War II, a somewhat peculiar character emerged from the ranks of the German air force. Hanns Scharff was his name. He had a gift that distinguished him from other stereotypically frightening interrogators.

Rather than using pain and fear to extract information from his prisoners beneath a blinding light, Scharff used the influence of kindness, humor, and a friendly environment. Scharff's method of gathering information was as calming as a soft wind on a bright day. And it worked.

Part 2: The Story

Picture a captured, worn-out, and disheartened enemy soldier sitting in a dark room with a single lightbulb throwing ominous shadows around him. In comes a man known all around the country as "The Master Interrogator."

Understandably terrified, the prisoner can only imagine what the diabolical interrogator will do to him to get his top-secret information. Hanns Scharff approaches the prisoner, but instead of tightening the restraints, he unties them. The next thing the prisoner knows, he's taking a leisurely stroll with Scharff in the beautiful German countryside. Talk about a plot twist. Taking his prisoners on private walks with no guards around was just one of Scharff's interrogating tactics. Scharff recognized that even the briefest moments of friendship could do wonders in loosening tongues.

But it didn't end there. Scharff had a few more tricks up his sleeve, or, in this case, his apron. One of his most famous tactics was making handmade meals for his prisoners. An interrogator cooking with his prisoners in a high-security prison would have made for a really entertaining reality cooking show. Imagine the prisoner's shock at learning that his captor wasn't only eager to learn his secrets but to tickle his tastebuds. Breaking through the walls between captor and captive, the aroma of freshly made bread drifting through the air became a sign of consolation and trust.

In addition to his aptitude for cooking, Scharff used the power of humor. He joked around with the prisoners and made them laugh. By Scharff's warmth and wit, which caught the captives off guard, they frequently found themselves saying more than they expected. Those must have been some pretty powerful knock-knock jokes. It was like the interrogations morphed into a casual conversation over a beer at a neighborhood bar.

Scharff told these jokes and stories over casual afternoon teas, and he even took the camaraderie a step further by taking the prisoners to the local zoo. Scharff's ability to disarm his captives with humor was a testament to the mighty power of kindness and empathy. These unconventional strategies helped humanize the prisoners and promote understanding between the enemies.

One of the reasons for this kind of treatment could be traced back to when Scharff was a subordinate in the army. He witnessed a prisoner being mistreated and pledged to behave differently if he was ever put into a position of leadership. Once he became an interrogator, he had the chance to act on this promise. He developed his own methods for interrogating.

Today, Scharff's technique is called, surprisingly enough, the Scharff Technique. It's made up of these four strategies:

1. Befriend the prisoner.
2. Let them talk, but don't press them for information.
3. Pretend to know everything.
4. Use confirmation/discontinuation.

Scharff ended up interrogating around 500 prisoners during his stint. Only about a couple dozen didn't give him any useful intel.

Part 3: The Breakdown

In a time when tensions seem to be running high, we can learn from Scharff's charm offensive. His ability to establish rapport and foster a welcoming environment serves as a reminder that kindness and empathy can bridge even the biggest gaps.

The heartwarming and kid-friendly interrogation techniques that Scharff used are proof of the effectiveness of kindness, empathy, and understanding. He proved that even under the worst of times, a little bit of humor and camaraderie can go a long way. He was able to extract knowledge through nature hikes, baking, humor, and companionship.

We can take inspiration from Scharff's legacy as we traverse the complexity of our own society by keeping in mind that treating others with kindness can result in much bigger benefits than hostility ever could.

CHAPTER 5:
DANCE 'TIL YOU DROP

Part 1: The Fact

In the summer of 1518, the people of Strasbourg, France, went about their normal lives when, all of a sudden, a weird phenomenon swept through the streets. It wasn't an unexpected siege by a group of hungry emu or a cluster of pop-ups selling mustache cups. It was the overwhelming need to dance.

Someone dropped the disco ball. As many as 400 people in Strasbourg found themselves uncontrollably dancing, and they couldn't stop. The tune they danced to was called the Dancing Plague of 1518.

Part 2: The Story

Between the months of July and September, between 50 and 400 people in Strasbourg were affected by an irrational dancing mania. There weren't even any viral dance videos around to make them do it, which would have made it all right. Even without the groovy music or the glittering disco balls, it appeared as though the town had been transformed into an impromptu disco marathon. People of all ages were affected by the overwhelming impulse to bust a move.

You may be asking yourself, "What's the big deal? It sounds like a lot of fun to dance." The catch, though, was that these poor people couldn't stop. They danced nonstop, day and night. The streets of Strasbourg were filled with twirling bodies, flailing limbs, and frenzied footwork. It must have looked like an unsynchronized flash mob, except for the fact that they kept dancing until they passed out from complete exhaustion. They would then get back up and continue to dance as if powered by invisible batteries. It was a continuous pattern of rhythmic madness.

The strange boogie fever outbreak perplexed the town's officials (who apparently never caught the dancing bug themselves somehow). They thought it could have been an omen, a supernatural spell, or maybe the reaction from a bad batch of pickled herring.

With no real explanation in sight, the town officials just figured the dancers would eventually tire out and stop on their own. To sort of help the dancers tire out a little more quickly, they built a town hall for the villagers to dance in, hired musicians to play for them, and, according to some stories, paid "strong men" to keep the tired dancers on their feet for as long as possible until they tired out.

An impromptu jam session couldn't last forever though. The dancing epidemic began to take its toll as the days progressed into weeks. The affected dancers became exhausted and dehydrated, which resulted in injuries and even deaths. Because the dancing just wouldn't stop, the town officials naturally decided the infected people had been consumed by a holy wrath. What else? They enforced penance on the town and banned music and dancing in public altogether.

There are a number of theories put out by historians and medical professionals on what caused this dance plague, but none of them can properly explain the phenomenon. Some say it might have been the result of a type of mass hysteria brought on by stress, religious zeal, or perhaps a combination of the two.

Others think the dancers may have eaten a grain contaminated with an uncommon fungus called ergot, which can cause hallucinations and spasms. Because ergot poisoning was known to happen in the area at the time, this it believed to be the most likely theory.

Part 3: The Breakdown

While we're not spontaneously breaking into dance marathons in the middle of the street without a phone close by to capture it all, there's something to be said about the contagious nature of human behavior. Ideas, beliefs, and emotions can easily sweep across societies, influencing our actions in ways we may not completely comprehend.

The Dancing Plague of 1518 serves as a reminder of the effectiveness of compassion and understanding. The townspeople may have made fun of or ridiculed the dancers because it was such an odd situation, but they instead decided to help and take care of them. They also recruited musicians to play for the dancers while providing medical help. It serves as a monument to the resilience of society and the human spirit.

CHAPTER 6:
REST IN PIZZA

Part 1: The Fact

In the small town of Ossineke, Michigan, a bizarre event took place in 1973 that gave the locals a sudden craving for a delicious slice of pizza- but hold the mushrooms, please.

The discovery of a possibly contaminated can of mushroom toppings led to a strange ceremony on a Michigan farm known as the Great Michigan Pizza Funeral, in which a local pizza company dumped thousands of frozen pizzas into an 18-foot grave.

Part 2: The Story

Local pizza maker Mario Fabbrini developed a solid reputation for his mouthwatering concoctions. He mastered the skill of creating delectable pizzas that could delight even the dullest of palates. But as luck would have it, trouble struck in the form of some tins of mushrooms swelling up. Swelled cans were bad news.

The Food and Drug Administration (FDA) discovered the batch contained a bacteria known as botulism, a food poisoning that can cause muscle weakness, low blood pressure, and sometimes even death. Unfortunately for Fabbrini, he used some of these bad mushrooms in his frozen pizzas. Out of concern for public health, the FDA immediately ordered the recall of the pizzas containing these potentially hazardous mushrooms.

When Fabbrini discovered he had to throw out almost 30,000 pizzas, he was horrified. It was a loss of $60,000, or nearly $380,000 in today's dollars. However, instead of just tossing the pizzas into the dumpster (or maybe ten dumpsters since one probably wouldn't be big enough),

Fabbrini decided to be a little more dramatic. He invited the residents of Ossineke to a funeral in his pizzas' honor. Hundreds of people showed up, including the local newspapers and even the governor, William G. Milliken. The governor delivered a brief homily "on courage in the face of tragedy" while dump trucks discarded the frozen pizzas into a large pit. Fabbrini even had his employees make pizzas for the guests as refreshments while they watched the tumbling waterfall of frozen dough. When the funeral was over, Fabbrini placed a two-color flower garland over the tomb: red gladioli for sauce and white carnations for cheese.

In the weeks after the cheesy funeral, it was discovered that the mushrooms in the pizzas weren't actually contaminated after all. Whoops. Fabbrini launched a court case that finally settled for $211,000. In a last stroke of bad luck, Papa Fabbrini Pizzas went out of business in the early 1980s. The pizza maker was forced to sell all of his assets for just $5,000.

Beyond the absurdity, however, the Great Michigan Pizza Funeral provides a fascinating window into the historical setting of the 1970s. Food safety and the need for stricter regulations were becoming a much bigger issue. The incident emphasized the role played by the FDA in protecting public health and the readiness of manufacturers like Fabbrini to comply with recall directives for the greater good.

Part 3: The Breakdown

As a result of rising globalization and complex supply chains, it's crucial to ensure the safety and quality of our food. The Great Michigan Pizza Funeral is a reminder of how important it is to put public health first and take necessary precautions to avoid any harm.

It's important to acknowledge the necessity for strict food safety laws and procedures given how connected the world is. By doing this, we can protect customer well-being and reduce the dangers brought on by complex supply networks.

The Great Michigan Pizza Funeral reinforces the idea that public health should always be a top priority in our globalized society by highlighting the importance of vigilance and the proactive measures needed to maintain high standards of food safety.

CHAPTER 7:
THE RIBBITING BATTERY

Part 1: The Fact

In the always intriguing world of scientific exploration came a peculiar experiment in the 1840s snatched right out of the everyday lily pond. A battery made up of frogs helped pave the way for further investigations into electricity.

While Benjamin Franklin decided to fly a kite in a lightning storm and risk electrocution, an Italian scientist decided to play it safe with frogs.

Part 2: The Story

A flurry of scientific advancements rocked the world in 1845. Among these included the use of anesthesia in childbirth for the first time, the patent of the rubber band, and the confirmation of the Doppler effect for sound waves.

One of the more unusual experiments in science at this time was the frog battery. Italian scientist and physiologist Carlo Matteucci decided to conduct an unusual experiment to develop a battery that could produce electricity. Maybe because he lived by a pond that was infested with too many frogs, he attempted to harness the power of electricity through frogs. Matteucci began his ribbiting experience with an open mind and a willingness to explore the limits of scientific understanding.

To build his frog battery, Matteucci connected 12 to 14 frog half-thighs together. The fact that he even thought of doing this in the first place is a weird event all in itself. With their bodies acting as the conductive medium, each frog performed the function of a single cell. These froggy cells could be linked together in a series configuration to generate power. Matteucci succeeded in developing an electrochemical battery that was powerful enough to break down potassium iodide. It was a literal biobattery.

Matteucci developed his frog battery on the heels of Italian scientist Luigi Galvani. In the late 1700s, Galvani found that dead frog legs could twitch when subjected to electrical currents. His research resulted in the development of the galvanic cell, a primitive battery type that eventually paved the way for Matteucci's frog battery. It looks like frogs were the go-to animals for all things electrical research.

So why did these Italian scientists choose frogs? Frogs actually possess a pretty peculiar trait that make them perfect for these experiments. They're very conductive due to the high amounts of electrolytes in their bodies. Frog muscles can also produce tiny electrical impulses, just like our own muscles can. Matteucci hoped to learn more about electricity by taking advantage of these special characteristics.

The frog battery became a popular instrument for early electrical research. It made it possible for researchers to examine and demonstrate different electrical events. Through his work, Matteucci ended up discovering the nerve's action potential, or nerve impulse. It was a powerful illustration of the powerful strength of one of nature's most ribbiting animals.

Part 3: The Breakdown

Today, we're still experimenting with unconventional energy sources while looking for environmentally acceptable and sustainable solutions. We're constantly motivated by nature's inventive methods, from solar energy to wind turbines. We're motivated, like Matteucci, to realize the untapped potential in the world.

The frog battery is a fun reminder of the value of imagination and creative problem-solving. We can be inspired by this froggy story in today's fast-paced world where creativity is highly rewarded. The most unlikely concepts can occasionally result in ground-breaking discoveries.

Let this story inspire you to embrace your own eccentric ideas. When you mix curiosity, a touch of silliness, and a willingness to push the boundaries of what's thought to be possible, you never know what exciting adventures may be in store. And who knows? Maybe the next big thing is waiting to be found just around the lily pad. Let's keep the frog thighs out of it, though. No one wants to see that.

CHAPTER 8:
HONEY, I'M SMOTHERED

Part 1: The Fact

An Egyptian pharaoh who inherited the throne at the not-so-pharaoh-ready age of six was known as one of Egypt's more demanding rulers. Apart from ordering the capture of a talented, dancing pygmy for his amusement, Pepi II also ordered his servants to keep the flies out of his sight.

Apparently, Pepi II didn't get the memo because flies were symbols of protection against misfortune and disease in ancient Egypt. Instead of welcoming this protection with a fly or two buzzing around his head, Pepi II did the opposite. To keep the flies away, he ordered his servants to attract the flies by coating themselves in globs of honey.

Part 2: The Story

In ancient Egypt, flies symbolized courage and tenacity. Stone carvings of flies have been found and dated back to approximately 3500 B.C. Golden flies would be awarded to soldiers who displayed bravery on the battlefield.

Fly amulets were also crafted from gold and silver. These were believed to protect the wearer from insect bites or to ward off flies.

No one knows why Pepi II didn't just wear a fly amulet to be fly-free, or maybe he somehow knew jewelry didn't actually ward off flies. Being a six-year-old, he probably found it more fun to watch people pour honey all over themselves anyway.

These human fly catchers covered themselves in honey from head to toe, like walking, talking human fly traps. The flies then naturally followed the servants and their sweet, sticky bodies. The flies flocked around them, keeping their annoying buzzing away from the revered presence of the pharaoh, unable to resist the draw of the honeyed attendants.

Being covered in honey could have been a pretty big deal for these servants. Sure, it was a sticky mess, but honey was extremely valuable in ancient Egypt. It served a variety of purposes and was considered a symbol of luxury and prosperity. The ancient Egyptians used honey as a natural sweetener and preservative.

Because honey was so highly valued, it was frequently used as money or presented to the gods as a sacred offering. Not to mention, honey bees were associated with the sun god Ra. According to Egyptian myth, honey bees were actually Ra's tears. Why they thought even a god would cry honey bees doesn't make too much sense.

Part 3: The Breakdown

Even though we no longer use such sticky tactics to ward off insects or protect our rulers, the desire to protect those in authority from harm remains in our subconscious.

Consider the security systems in place today and the efforts made to preserve the reputation and safety of powerful people. Although we may not use honey as a coat but just to coat our pancakes, the point is the same.

This weird event from ancient Egypt is also a reminder that sometimes our approaches to a problem might be kind of bizarre. Even though we may find the concept of human fly traps amusing, it's important to recognize our ancestors' inventiveness and innovation. They handled difficulties with a mix of creativity and humor, coming up with imaginative solutions.

It's an important lesson to remember that occasionally the most unlikely and outlandish strategies can produce unanticipated benefits.

CHAPTER 9:
THE WILD WILD CAMELS

Part 1: The Fact

A portrait of the Wild West usually contains images of cowboys on galloping horses and lawless bandits riding across vast landscapes. There's another element to this era in the mid-1800s that hasn't often been included in this picture.

The Wild West was full of camels. These magnificent animals, distinguished by their humps and odd sideways swaying walk, weren't indigenous to the area but were introduced to the United States by the U.S. Army. They helped push the era along much more than the horse or the mule.

Part 2: The Story

The American West was a vast, uncharted frontier in 1856. In order to navigate this difficult terrain, the U.S. Army came up with a brilliant idea. Instead of relying on slow horses and mules to carry their heavy loads, they decided the camel would be much more helpful. As a result, the Army launched the United States Camel Corps Experiment.

The Army imported around 70 camels from the Middle East to Texas, both dromedaries (camels with a single hump) and Bactrian camels (camels with two humps). Camels could endure longer travel times than horses and mules without the need for regular water breaks. For example, a camel could travel with a heavy burden in two days when it would take a mule to do in five. Also, it took six camels nearly two days less time to do a task that 12 horses could do.

The camels' grand debut in the American Southwest sparked quite a commotion among the locals. They must have been pretty confused seeing these strange animals gallivanting by with their long craning necks and their swaying humps. The animals weren't exactly too popular. They constantly smelled and tended to spit a lot. But despite their terrible personal hygiene, camels proved to be very helpful for the Army's exploration missions. The animals carried bulky supplies and equipment and even acted as mounts for the soldiers.

The camels would soon be out of a job, however. The Camel Corps Experiment eventually came to an end in 1863 because of the onset of the Civil War. Some of the camels were sold, while others were released into the Texas, Arizona, and California deserts. With their newfound independence, the camels flourished in their new surroundings. They did a remarkable job of adjusting to the rough landscapes.

Unfortunately, the wild camel herds gradually disappeared as the 20th century went on. They had to deal with a variety of difficulties, such as habitat degradation and hunting. The last of the wild camels disappeared from the American Southwest by the early 1900s, leaving behind a legacy that is as strange as it is fascinating.

Part 3: The Breakdown

Even though we might not have any roaming camels in our backyards, this odd story shows us important lessons about adaptability and the unanticipated results of human endeavors. The U.S. Army's camel experiment reminds us that innovative thinking, accepting ideas, and taking chances can occasionally create surprisingly positive outcomes. It challenges us to embrace our inner wackiness and not to be afraid to attempt something new, even if it initially looks a little absurd.

The tale of these wild camels also serves as a reminder of the value of environmental stewardship. We're reminded of the fragile balance between human activities and the natural environment by the disappearance of the camel herds. It makes us think about the long-term effects of our choices and the necessity of preserving and protecting the distinctive ecosystems all around us.

So the next time you find yourself out in the American Southwest with a couple of camels at your side, be mindful of where you leave them because they could very well repopulate the Wild Wild West once again.

CHAPTER 10:
ALEXANDER THE BURIED

Part 1: The Fact

Alexander the Great was considered to be, well, great. He was a king of ancient Macedonia and Persia who built the largest empire in the ancient world. That's why it was a shock when the ruler suddenly died at the age of 32.

Little is known about how Alexander died, but historians now believe he may have been accidentally buried alive.

Part 2: The Story

It all began with the unfortunate turn of events surrounding Alexander's health. What really happened during his dying days has long baffled historians and scientists. At age 32, the powerful commander suddenly passed away in Babylon.

Historians have been trying to figure out what happened to him for decades. Many theories have been talked about, from typhoid disease or poison to alcoholism or malaria. There's one particular theory that stands out from the rest, and that would be Guillain-Barré Syndrome.

Guillain-Barré Syndrome is a rare neurological condition that affects the peripheral nervous system. It can result in weakness, numbness, and, in extreme cases, paralysis. Experts speculate that Alexander the Great may have succumbed to this strange ailment six days before his actual burial. As a result, the ancient Macedonian king was probably still alive when his devoted yet oblivious subjects prepared his body for burial.

According to legend, Alexander's illness started after a wild night of drinking where he downed 12 pints of wine. The next morning, Alexander woke up complaining of aches and exhaustion. That should have been a clue to maybe take a day off from conquering, but he decided to go ahead and conquer another 12 pints of wine.

The following day, Alexander began to experience severe abdomen aches and a fever that only kept getting worse. After eight days, the great leader was bedridden, in severe pain, and progressively losing his capacity to move. Soon, he could only blink his eyes and twitch his hands. The king was declared dead by the end of the 11th day, although his staff claimed he was conscious up until the very end.

At the time, doctors didn't check the pulse when checking if someone was dead or alive. Instead, doctors only looked for indicators that the patient was still breathing. If Alexander had indeed suffered from Guillain-Barré Syndrome, then his whole body could have been paralyzed. The paralysis would have restricted his respiratory muscles so that his breaths were so small that they'd be undetectable by doctors. Greek scholars did note that Alexander's body never decayed in the days following his passing. But they buried him anyway. Someone's getting fired.

Part 3: The Breakdown

Despite how bizarre and grim this historical event may seem, it offers us a fascinating look at both the historical event and Alexander the Great's life, which has long been shrouded in mystery. It sheds light on the belief system of the time, in which the distinction between life and death was less distinct than it is today. It's evidence of the anxiety and perplexity that might develop when confronted with the unknowable and the boundaries of medical understanding.

The tale of Alexander's unintentional burial serves as a reminder of the value of scientific discovery and understanding. Because diseases and afflictions were frequently cloaked in mystery in the past, strange occurrences like these could result from a lack of knowledge and understanding.

With a better understanding of numerous illnesses and ailments, modern medicine has advanced significantly. Alexander's story serves as a reminder to value the advancements we've made and the ongoing work required to increase our understanding in the quest for better healthcare.

CHAPTER 11: SMART DUNCE CAPS

Part 1: The Fact

The towering, pointed, wizard-like dunce cap that we now connect with mischievous or not-so-bright kids sitting in the corner of the classroom in shame once stood for something else entirely.

Back in the Middle Ages, intellectuals would wear these pointy hats as a crazy fashion statement because they thought the hat's pointed design could somehow function as a reverse funnel to bring knowledge down into the brain. It looks like they desperately needed to wear these hats because, with this kind of thinking, they didn't seem to be all too bright. As a result, what we now refer to as the shameful dunce cap was once considered a sign of high intelligence.

Part 2: The Story

The dunce cap started out as a symbol of academic success. It was worn by respected people who had made outstanding intellectual achievements. Imagine strolling down the street wearing a pointed hat that gave off an air of sophistication. People would respect you because they believed the cone-shaped headdress meant you had tremendous wisdom and wit.

You might be wondering how exactly dunce caps changed from being a symbol of brightness to, well, not so brightness. Here's where the interesting fact really shines. Enter John Duns Scotus, a philosopher from Scotland. He was well-known for having a keen mind and intellectual insight. When he was most likely in his 20s, he enlisted as a Franciscan priest in 1291. He later achieved greatness as a philosopher, linguist, theologian, and thinker of metaphysics.

During his studies, Scotus developed a complex philosophical justification for the presence of a metaphysical God as opposed to a tangible "Man in the Sky." He also believed that the Virgin Mary herself was conceived without sin. Scotus became known as "The Subtle Doctor" because of the complexity of his beliefs. His teachings became known as "Scotism," and his followers became known as "Dunsmen" or "Dunces." They all wore these pointed hats. For whatever reason, Scotus loved to wear these hats. It's been said that he inspired the popular image of wizards wearing similar pointed caps.

Scotus' theories, however, eventually lost favor with other philosophers over time, even after his death. His incredibly analytical works and convoluted logic were eventually seen as too sophisticated and at odds with the more humanistic ideas developing with the emerging Renaissance thought.

The remaining Dunsmen, who persisted in focusing on Scotist philosophy, started to be seen as hopelessly behind the times or just plain stupid. As a result, the Dunsmen gained a reputation for being stupid, and their pointy hats came to represent this unpleasant new reputation. As a result, people were ordered to wear the cap as a punishment for their supposed intellectual inadequacies. It eventually became a tool for public humiliation.

Part 3: The Breakdown

Even though the dunce cap may appear to be a thing of the past, we can still learn from its strange journey. It serves as a reminder that opinions and perceptions can evolve. Our knowledge and opinions change, just as the dunce cap changed from a sign of brilliance to one of foolishness. We should always approach people with an open mind, understanding that our initial impressions might not always be correct.

The dunce cap also serves as a reminder of the influence of labels. Being called a "dunce" was a way to exclude and humiliate someone in public. We should be careful about the labels we give people or groups in the modern world because they might reinforce prejudices and prevent us from seeing their genuine value.

So keep the story of the wise dunce caps in mind the next time you see a quirky hat or come across a historically bizarre incident. Embrace the laughter, strive for greater understanding, and work to uncover the fascinating facts that make our world both joyful and odd.

CHAPTER 12:
THE MAN WHO ATE EVERYTHING

Part 1: The Fact

In the vibrant streets of 1790s France lived a man known simply as Tarrare. Tarrare wasn't your typical Frenchman. He was a man with an unquenchable appetite that even the hungriest of us couldn't match. Because of his infamous insatiable appetite, Tarrare was known as "The Insatiable Glutton."

Part 2: The Story

The story of Tarrare begins with a rather unfortunate start. He had a huge appetite as a young boy that was nothing short of amazing. His poor parents just weren't able to satisfy his insatiable appetite. As a result, a teenage Tarrare found himself kicked out of his family's home and forced to scavenge for food on the streets. Tarrare soon found himself traveling with a colorful crew of robbers and set out on a journey through the French countryside. Now, one might wonder how a man with such a huge appetite could live on such a journey. This is where things really start to get strange.

Tarrare caught the attention of a traveling showman who was an expert at spectacle and trickery. Realizing the crowd-drawing spectacle that Tarrare's unique abilities could provide for him, the showman invited him to be his warm-up act. Tarrare's role in the show was ingesting corks, stones, and even live animals. The crowd was in awe of his most incredible achievement: consuming a whole basket of apples. His massive, deformed jaw would swing open so wide that he could pour the entire basket full of apples down his throat and hold a dozen of them in his cheeks like a chipmunk.

Tarrare traveled to the magnificent city of Paris after word of his exceptional talents spread there. He established himself as a well-known street performer. People flocked to watch him eat enormous amounts of meat in one sitting. It was rumored that Tarrare could eat entire carcasses, bones and all, without showing any signs of reluctance or indigestion. Witnesses claimed they saw him eat a live cat, leaving just the skeleton. One time, he allegedly swallowed a live eel without chewing it.

Tarrare had a tremendous appetite, but he was surprisingly physically weak and fragile. Adding to this confusing image, he had folds of extra skin just hanging off his stomach when he wasn't full. His insides seemed to be an unending void that could never be filled. The young man weighed just 100 pounds and was always tired. He always showed every possible sign of undernourishment despite always stuffing everything in sight into his mouth.

Tarrare later decided to give up life as a street performer and enlisted in the French military. Because he required quadruple the rations compared to the other soldiers, the military quickly threw him out. One of the generals had an idea, though. He put a document inside a wooden box, had Tarrare eat it, and then waited for it to pass through Tarrare's body. Then he had a very unfortunate soldier clean through Tarrare's mess to fish out the box to see if the document could still be read. It worked, and Tarrare was given his first mission as a spy. He was to sneak past enemy lines as a German peasant to deliver a top-secret message to a captured French colonel. Well, pretending to be a German peasant didn't exactly work out because Tarrare couldn't speak German. He was caught.

By the end of his short life, Tarrare had tried everything to get rid of his insatiable hunger. He tried wine vinegar, tobacco pills, and every other medicine imaginable at the time. After being accused of eating a 14-month-old baby, Tarrare pretty much disappeared from the public eye. He passed away at age 26 from tuberculosis. Doctors performed an autopsy on him and found his stomach so massive that it nearly filled his entire abdominal cavity.

Part 3: The Breakdown

One can't help but make comparisons to the era of viral videos and reality TV when thinking about the similarities to our modern society. We're always looking for the next shocking show to satisfy our obsession with the extraordinary. Tarrare's peculiar career serves as a reminder that our craving for amusement, even when it seems silly, has existed since the beginning of time.

Tarrare's story also serves as a warning against excess. His enormous appetite and amazing abilities may astound us, but they also make us think about the value of moderation and balance. Tarrare's ravenous appetite ultimately brought about his demise, as it caused him to experience serious health problems. As we ponder Tarrare's life's peculiarities, let's keep in mind the historical lessons that are tucked away in the pages. Value the beauty of human diversity and the quirks that make us unique. Let's also aim for balance and make sure that our wants and desires don't swallow us whole.

CHAPTER 13:
THE STICKY TSUNAMI

Part 1: The Fact

Boston had its own sort of Pompeii moment on a warmer-than-usual day in January 1919. Instead of lava washing over the city, what eyewitnesses say was a 40-foot wave of goo swept through the Boston streets. It was a molasses tsunami.

On that fateful day, a giant 58-foot-tall cast-iron tank packed to the brim with sweet, gooey molasses erupted, unleashing a torrent of stickiness upon the unprepared city. The Great Molasses Flood of 1919 turned the streets of Boston into a sticky and surreal nightmare.

Part 2: The Story

The United States Industrial Alcohol Company owned the tank that exploded. They had been told that the tank, filled with a whopping 2.5 million gallons of crude molasses that could fill eight Olympic-sized swimming pools, was leaking. Their response was to paint the tank brown to hide the dripping molasses. Nothing good can happen from ignoring a warning about a giant tub of sticky syrup.

Storing a tank of over two million gallons of molasses might seem like an unusually large amount, but it wasn't unusual for Boston. The Massachusetts city had long been a major molasses center and was a significant player in the rum trade. Molasses, the substance left over after sugar cane is boiled to extract sugar, was an important ingredient in rum.

On January 15th, the bolts holding the bottom of the tank exploded. The hot molasses rushed out at a speeding 35 miles per hour, sweeping away the nearby freight cars.

As the tank exploded, it unleashed a tsunami of molasses that surged through the streets like a scene out of a wild movie. It literally knocked over the local firehouse and then pushed over the support beams for the elevated train line. It was like a bizarre molasses rollercoaster, only not exactly very fun.

The molasses deluge destroyed everything in its path. Buildings collapsed like weak cardboard boxes because the sweet tide's unrelenting fury was greater than their structural strength.

Horses, unfortunate victims of the gooey flood, were trapped in the sticky sea. Chaos reigned as people tried to free themselves from the clutches of the rapidly solidifying molasses, with its sugary aroma now tinged with danger. Around 150 people were injured, not to mention several cats and dogs.

The molasses flood had a long-lasting impact on Boston. Residents stated that for decades, the streets still had a faint molasses odor on hot summer days.

Part 3: The Breakdown

The Great Molasses Flood provides us with some intriguing perspectives on history and the human condition. It serves as a reminder that even the most unanticipated happenings can have significant repercussions. It teaches us always to be ready for the unexpected and never undervalue the strength of nature or the potential threats hidden in commonplace items.

This sticky mess is a reflection of the world we live in today as well. Even while there may not be molasses tsunamis flooding through our streets, it serves as a warning that unforeseen events can interrupt our lives at any time. We must be watchful and adjust to the changing times, whether it's a natural calamity, a sudden change in technology, or a global pandemic.

So let's appreciate the oddities and unexpectedness of history as we reflect on the Great Molasses Flood of 1919. Let's take the lessons it teaches and keep in mind a sense of humor even when things are difficult. Perhaps one day, we'll be telling tales of the great toilet paper scarcity to future generations. After all, just like a tsunami of molasses through the streets of Boston, life is full of unforeseen shocks.

CHAPTER 14: TURKEY WORSHIP

Part 1: The Fact

The concept of Thanksgiving didn't exist in the world of the ancient Mayans 2,000 years ago, but turkeys still played an important role in their society.

It turns out that the wonderful and plump turkeys we now associate with Thanksgiving feasts were originally thought to be supernatural beings. The Mayans worshiped and revered these birds as gods.

Part 2: The Story

The Mayans flourished in the lush jungles of Mesoamerica and held a deep respect for the natural world and its species. They all had a special place in their stomachs, or hearts, for turkeys. But the Mayans were fascinated by these birds for more than simply their delicious meat. They believed these birds were the earthly vessels of the gods themselves.

The turkey possessed a majestic aura that the Mayans found inspiring thanks to its gorgeous plumage and regal behavior. These turkeys the Mayans were familiar with weren't exactly like the modern-day turkeys that we're so accustomed to. Domesticated versions of these turkeys are the ones that wind up on our holiday plates today.

The ocellated turkey was the species of turkey that inhabited the Yucatán Peninsula that the Mayans respected as gods. They're far more attractive than our overweight chicken friends. They looked a little more like peacocks with their magnificent bronze, blue, and green feathers, vivid blue heads with wart-like, orangey nodules, dark red feet, and a tail with eyelike markings. To the Mayans, these characteristics gave turkeys the appearance of living representations of the gods who ruled over nature.

The eyes on these turkeys' tails were thought to be intelligent and possess the knowledge of everything. The Mayans also regarded the turkey as a divine messenger who possessed extraordinary abilities and could cast spells at night and in dreams.

The birds indicated personal power and wealth and were often owned to show one's prominence in society. Turkeys served as symbols in the Mayan calendar and were even buried with the deceased.

The Mayans honored these turkeys with temples decorated with feathers from the bird, rituals honoring the turkey gods, and even idols in the form of turkeys. The birds were thought to be able to converse with the gods and serve as a bridge between the divine and human realms.

The Mayans frequently sacrificed turkeys as part of their religious ceremonies in the hope that by doing so, they would please the gods and secure abundant harvests and good fortune. Maybe if the Australian farmers revered the emu the same way, they wouldn't have had so many problems.

Part 3: The Breakdown

Although we no longer revere turkeys as gods, the tale of Mayan turkey worship serves as a reminder of our interest in nature and desire to understand our place in it. Today, we still have a great deal of regard for animals, not as gods, but rather as fellow members of the earth. We're aware of how crucial it is to maintain environmental balance and biodiversity.

We're equally as enthralled by the wonder and beauty of the natural world as the Mayans were, from the vibrant birds in our gardens to the magnificent wildlife roaming in other regions.

The Mayan practice of turkey worship also shows us the significance of cultural diversity and the depth of various religious traditions. It serves as a reminder to treat unknown cultures and traditions with respect and curiosity, understanding that even if they appear strange or unconventional at first, there's wisdom to be found in other people's beliefs.

Take some time to appreciate the humble turkey as you sit down to your next Thanksgiving meal. Consider the transformation these birds underwent from being worshipped as gods to serving as the focal point of our holiday feasts. During that period of reflection, you can discover a stronger bond with earlier civilizations and a fresh respect for the complex story of human history.

CHAPTER 15:
DOG LOVER EXTREME

Part 1: The Fact

In the land of northwestern India near the Arabian Sea, a ruler lived like no other in the early 1900s. Muhammed Mahabat Khan III was the last ruler of Junagadh from 1911 to 1948. He holds the distinct honor in Indian history for his extraordinary commitment to the protection of a truly magnificent animal, the Asiatic lion.

However, this weird historical fact has more to do with canines than felines. Muhammed had a unique and quirky fascination that would make anyone wag their tail in wonder. He loved his dogs more than anything, all 800 of them.

Part 2: The Story

Picture a palace that would put even the fanciest doggy daycare to shame. You'd find Muhammed in the middle of it. He had a deep affection for his 800 furry companions. You may think that was 799 dogs too many, but this Maharaja wasn't your typical dog lover. Each of his fluffy companions had the privilege of having its own private room, complete with all the canine comforts a dog could dream of. That must have been a pretty big palace. Hopefully, no one with any fur allergies stepped inside.

In true regal style, each dog had its own attendant. These devoted servants made sure the dogs led lives of pure luxury. They were the ideal dog caregivers, providing them with scrumptious goodies and plenty of hours of belly rubs and fur-stroking. It sounds like a doggone dream come true.

Muhammed even spent thousands on birthday parties and wedding ceremonies for his favorites. To turn up the luxury even more, each dog had its own phone in its room. With only a single ring, they could issue a command or even plan a howling party with their canine friends.

Even though Muhammed's affection for dogs may seem a little too much even for the average avid dog lover, it illustrates the strong bond between a monarch and his followers, even if those subjects happened to have tails.

It's understandable why these stories, which showcase the quirks and oddities of historical personalities, have survived through the ages. But this story isn't only about royal eccentricities and extravagant dogs.

Muhammed's commitment to protecting the majestic and threatened Asiatic lion is evidence of his compassion for all living things. He was a pioneer in understanding the value of preserving endangered species and the delicate balance of our planet's ecosystems by fighting for the survival of these stunning animals. Muhammed surely would have invited a few lions over to live with him if he didn't already have a few hundred dogs running up some very high room service bills.

Part 3: The Breakdown

Environmental conservation and the preservation of endangered species remain important issues for us today. The story of Muhammed Mahabat Khan III and his amazing devotion to animals serves as a reminder that, despite the quirkiness of our approaches, we can all make a difference.

The Maharaja's fondness for his animal companions tells us about the strength of love and friendship. Since the beginning of time, dogs have been faithful companions because they're devoted and affectionate animals. They remind us of the happiness that comes from the straightforward joys that come from being with animals. Our furry pals may bring comfort, joy, and a warm hug at the end of a long day in a world that can frequently feel chaotic and unexpected.

After reading about Muhammad's story, we're left with a wag in our tails and a smile on our faces thanks to his special brand of dog love and animal activism. May we all be motivated by his story to embrace the value of conservation, value the company of our animal friends, and never underestimate the healing power of a belly massage.

CHAPTER 16:
THE WAR ON CATS

Part 1: The Fact

There are two types of people, right? Those who love cats and those who just plain don't. One can argue there are many more people in the first category these days, but that wasn't so in the 13th century. Basically everybody was on the "we despise cats" side, and it was all thanks to one certain person who shall not remain nameless.

Throughout history, some people have gone a little too far in their treatment of cats. Pope Gregory IX was one of them. Believing cats to pretty much be the devil in a fur coat, he declared an official war on these furry little companions.

Part 2: The Story

It all started in 1232 during Pope Gregory IX's reign as Pope. People during this time period believed in a lot of very weird and completely unrealistic things. Unfortunately, cats were caught in the proverbial cat hairs of human paranoia during this time. There were rumors that cats were connected to witchcraft and devilry. Pope Gregory became caught up in the wave of cat phobia too.

According to legend, the Pope came to believe that cats were somehow connected to the devil. A string of unlucky occurrences happened to support this belief. Europe was battling the plague during Gregory's rule, and many people thought cats were the source of the disease. What nobody knew at the time, the real cause of the plague was fleas on rats, but cats got the blame.

In a move that baffled many, Pope Gregory declared a holy war against cats. He issued a papal bull, or an official decree, that declared all cats were diabolical creatures and should be exterminated. The faithful were encouraged to hunt down and exterminate every single cat they saw.

Even though declaring war on cats was simply ridiculous, people were all for it. Cats were brutally hunted and exterminated all over Europe. Instead of eliminating the plague like they hoped, it just got worse. The rat population grew without cats around to hunt them, and this accelerated the spread of the plague that people were trying to stop.

Instead of realizing their mistake, people then started to believe that the plague grew worse because Satan was so angry with the deaths of so many of his cats. It was a no-win-no-win situation.

Part 3: The Breakdown

After hearing about this wacky war, it's easy to shake your head in disbelief and wonder what on earth was Pope Gregory thinking. The many advantages of having cats as pets have been demonstrated by modern research. Their presence can lower blood pressure, alleviate stress, and endlessly entertain us with their amusing and super cute antics. If only Pope Gregory had realized how much happiness and solace cats provide. Or maybe he was allergic to them, and raging war on them was the only thing he could think of to get rid of them.

This odd historical event also serves as a warning against the perils of ignorance and superstition. It's amazing to see how incorrect assumptions and unsubstantiated rumors can influence irrational behavior, even from the high levels of authority.

It's important to keep in mind that even though we may chuckle at the ridiculousness of the cat crusade, such events can have far-reaching effects.

CHAPTER 17:
HUBERTA THE HIPPO

Part 1: The Fact

Huberta was a hippo on a mission, or she just wanted to get her steps in. In 1928, Huberta left her watering hole and began what ended up being a three-year-long journey through the South African wilderness.

This hippo's seemingly endless journey caught the world's attention and created a newfound love for the hippo, quickly causing Huberta to become a national icon and symbol of hope.

Part 2: The Story

Huberta's story begins in South Africa. During one fine day in her beautiful watering hole, she decided that her life in the river was just too boring for her adventurous spirit. Without further ado, she bid farewell to her fellow hippos and embarked on a trip that would ultimately take her 1,000 miles away from her home.

With the confidence only a hippo could have, Huberta left her watering hole in the St. Lucia Estuary in KwaZulu-Natal and rambled across the beautiful South African countryside. She crossed wide fields and thick forests and quickly caught the attention of the locals.

People from all walks of life excitedly anticipated the wandering hippo's arrival in their cities and villages as word of her journey spread like wildfire. Huberta became sort of like a local celebrity as people flocked to see the amazing creature along her path.

Huberta had quite the adventure. She swam across rivers, traveled across vast plains, and even crossed highways, indifferent to the chaos she caused all around her. She crossed the Black Umfolozi River, went swimming at the Durban beach, had a moonlit bath in the pond of a monastery garden, and even once stopped a train by dozing off on the tracks until the locomotive's cattle guard had to wake her up.

When she was about 125 miles from her home, Huberta once spent some time relaxing in a lagoon along the Mhlanga River and astonished visitors at the Beachwood Golf Course. The locals treated her like a queen and even fed her snacks. She calmly strolled around, winning the hearts of everyone she came across.

It wasn't just the public that found Huberta's quest so fascinating. The media also became obsessed with this roving hippo's charm. Reporters eagerly followed her every move as newspapers extensively covered her story. Huberta became a beloved character in South African mythology as a result of her exploits.

Despite all eyes on her, nobody really knew where Huberta was going or why she was traveling. Some thought she was hunting for a long-lost love. Others believed she was making a pilgrimage to the home of her ancestors. Another theory was that she was trying to get to the coast to live in the salt water ocean.

Huberta's journey ultimately came to an end in March 1931. She had traversed around 122 rivers and finally settled in the Eastern Cape in the Keiskamma River. Unfortunately, she was killed by a group of hunters who later claimed they had no idea she was the famous hippo. South Africans mourned her passing by writing sympathy cards and poetry in her honor.

Part 3: The Breakdown

Huberta's travels had a significant historical influence on the people of South Africa. She rose to prominence as a symbol of fortitude and the spirit of adventure, serving as a constant reminder to everyone to occasionally leave the comforts of familiarity and embrace the uncharted.

Huberta's story reminds us there's a vast world out there waiting to be explored and that sometimes we simply need to take a leap of faith and follow our instincts as this brave hippo did.

Huberta's journey is a testament to the strength of togetherness and its capacity to unite individuals. Her tale demonstrates that despite the current state of affairs, we can still find common ground and unite behind something as straightforward as a wandering hippo. It's evidence of the resilient nature of people and the happiness that comes from bonding with others. Let her story encourage us to embrace our own inner wanderer and embark on our own unique adventure.

CHAPTER 18:
ELECTRIFYING FASHIONS

Part 1: The Fact

There have been some very odd trends in the ever-changing world of fashion throughout history. People have always found ways to display their personality through clothing, from wigs that reached staggering heights to dresses so wide they required doorways to be widened.

In the 1770s, one such odd fashion appeared on the chic Parisian streets, involving an electrifying adornment that was both trendy and, well, shocking.

Part 2: The Story

The 1770s buzzed with excitement over the latest fashion trend in the form of the ladies' lightning rod cap. Fashion-forward women began wearing caps with metallic threads that were cleverly connected to a cord that gracefully dragged along the ground as they strolled through the city streets.

Unbelievably, the general belief was that these lightning rod coverings would act as a safety precaution during thunderstorms. The concept behind this electrified accessory was that when worn, the string attached to the metallic threads would serve as a lightning rod, securely guiding any electrical bolts away from the wearer. Before we laugh too hard since we now know the exact opposite would happen, let's acknowledge the ingenuity and imagination that went into this odd fashion choice.

One of Benjamin Franklin's students, Jacques Barbeu-Dubourg, developed another electrifying accessory in the form of a lightning-rod umbrella. Imagine being protected from both the rain and Mother Nature's electrical displays as you strolled down the Champs-Élysées on a rainy day. In his design, Barbeu-Dubourg included a metal pole that served as a lightning rod and a silver braid that gracefully dangled along the ground, ready to deflect any potentially harmful charges.

Let's now take a brief break to consider the sheer audacity and optimism that motivated these fashion trends. In the 18th century, which was a time of scientific advancement and enlightenment, individuals were enthralled by their growing grasp of electricity. The lightning rod, a groundbreaking creation that Benjamin Franklin is credited with creating, aroused widespread interest and caught the minds of both intellectuals and common people.

We can't help but smile at the lovely fusion of whimsy and scientific passion in the instance of the lightning rod caps and umbrellas. Parisians embraced these odd dress choices as a way to show that they were participating in the intellectual atmosphere of the day. It was a cheerful attempt to tame the natural world through clothing and a whimsical manifestation of society's preoccupation with electricity.

Part 3: The Breakdown

Although these trends are extremely absurd, it's crucial to recognize that their foundations were faulty scientific beliefs. A simple attachment can't cleanly redirect lightning due to its great power and unpredictable nature. Nevertheless, we may learn a lot from this peculiar incident in the history of fashion.

It serves as a reminder of our urge to learn more about and understand the world around us, even if that involves going into strange and absurd places. The lightning rod hats and umbrellas were evidence of our predecessors' unquenchable curiosity and eagerness to try out novel ideas, even when they were absurd.

We can also draw a comparison between the lightning rod fashion trend and the state of the world now. It's crucial to approach new ideas with a healthy dose of skepticism and critical thinking at a time when scientific and technological breakthroughs appear to be happening at an unparalleled rate. We must be critical and question the truthfulness of theories and trends that catch our interest, just as the lightning rod caps and umbrellas turned out to be nothing more than attractive dreams.

CHAPTER 19:
THE MOLDY BREAD CURE

Part 1: The Fact

If you were to take a stroll through the busy streets of ancient Egypt, you would be awestruck by the majestic pyramids, the mysterious Sphinxes, and of course the servants who were covered in honey.

You might also come across a wise Egyptian healer slapping a piece of bread on a rotting wound. They weren't using the bread as a bandage. They were using the mold on the bread as an antibiotic. Sure, both of these situations sound weird to us today. However, using moldy bread as an antibiotic was a cutting-edge medical procedure for the ancient Egyptians.

Part 2: The Story

The ancient Egyptians actually found out about the concept of antibiotics thousands of years before their modern discovery. Why no one discovered antibiotics between these two periods is quite unfortunate to those who could have used them. Despite their poor understanding of microorganisms due to their tendency to concentrate on bigger objects like pyramids, the ancient Egyptians discovered that moldy bread had certain properties that could help treat infections.

In these ancient times, when a noble warrior came home from battle with a serious injury, the Egyptian healers would run to their kitchens and scan their pantries for any moldy bread. They found that some molds, especially those that grew on bread, had antibiotic characteristics that could treat illnesses. If a healer ran a side business as a baker, they hit the jackpot.

They noticed that bread left out for a long time would start to produce a fuzzy, greenish-blue substance that was actually a type of mold. Little did they know that this mold teemed with the extraordinary antibiotic called penicillin.

After randomly deciding to cover blistering wounds with this greenish-blue fuzz, the healers began harnessing the power of this mold to combat infections. In the hopes it would work, they carefully scraped off the mold and applied it to the affected region.

The success rates weren't perfect, as you might expect. In some cases, the moldy bread treatment was effective in curing wounds and warding off any lingering bad spirits. Unfortunately, there were times when it didn't work, leaving the poor patient to their fate. The ancient Egyptians didn't understand that it was the properties inside the mold and not just the mold itself that was doing the curing.

It's amazing to see how inventive and determined the ancient Egyptians were to develop cures for illnesses. Although they lacked our modern scientific understanding but had a breakthrough when it came to getting rid of their flies, they used observation, experimentation, and intuition to discover the therapeutic benefits of moldy bread. Their persistence helped pave the way for later advances in medicine, which ultimately resulted in the modern era's discovery of antibiotics.

Part 3: The Breakdown

Despite the fact that we thankfully no longer use moldy bread as medicine, we can learn a lot from the Egyptian physicians' curiosity. They looked for answers to urgent issues and refused to accept the status quo.

It's easy to ignore the treasures that are right at our fingertips in today's fast-paced world. We may nurture an open mind and embrace the uncharted possibilities that are all around us by embracing the spirit of ancient Egypt. Who knows what clever answers might be hiding in the most unlikely places?

This weird event serves as a reminder that the most unlikely circumstances frequently lead to advancement and discovery. We must keep an open mind to unanticipated advances in science and medicine, just as the ancient Egyptians did when they accidentally discovered the healing powers of moldy bread. The most commonplace and unimpressive beginnings can lead to the most amazing breakthroughs.

CHAPTER 20:
THE TAJ BAMBOO

Part 1: The Fact

People from all over the world have been captivated by the Taj Mahal's brilliant white marble, complex sculptures, and magnificent domes. It had a slightly different appearance during World War II, however. In order to protect the Seventh Wonder of the World, the Taj Mahal was covered in bamboo to confuse any enemy bombers flying overhead.

Part 2: The Story

As the war raged on in the 1940s, India found itself caught in the crossfire and faced the constant danger of bomb threats. The government was committed to preventing any potential damage to their cherished Taj Mahal.

It was difficult to come up with a plan to protect such a magnificent structure from the ominous bombs falling from the skies. They ended up coming up with a very clever scheme involving an unexpected solution in the form of bamboo. It was time for the Taj Mahal to put on a vanishing act.

The Taj Mahal's dome was meticulously covered in bamboo scaffolding by the Indian government to properly conceal its true identity from any prying eyes in the sky. It was like wrapping an elaborate bamboo-shaped cloak around a giant to pass it off as an ordinary stick or witnessing a peacock dressing up as a turkey to avoid attention. Imagine the wonder of seeing one of the most stunning structures in the world converted into a seemingly uninteresting pile of bamboo. It must have been a sight to behold.

The whimsical plan actually worked. The Taj Mahal remained unharmed throughout the war. The enemy bombers, fooled by the disguise, never thought in a million years that beneath those layers of bamboo was a treasure of architectural brilliance. The Taj Mahal survived the turbulent times and emerged unharmed, its beauty still intact. Because the plan was so effective, it was actually done twice again when India fought wars against Pakistan in 1965 and 1971.

Part 3: The Breakdown

This story may seem like a silly anecdote from the past, but it actually has a deeper meaning that still applies today. It serves as a reminder of the value of imagination, flexibility, and unconventional thinking. We frequently come across unforeseen hardships during difficult times, just like the people who lived through World War II. The story of the Taj Mahal's vanishing act serves as a reminder that sometimes, the most unusual ideas might end up saving the day.

This weird event also draws attention to the value of protecting cultural artifacts and legacy. The authorities knew the value of the Taj Mahal and did everything they could think of to protect it, no matter what it was. They realized this amazing structure was more than just a work of art and that it was also a representation of India's history and pride in one's country. In the same way, it's important to continue the cultural heritage that's represented by our modern-day landmarks.

We can learn from the inventiveness shown in this weird incident as we live through the trying times we live in today when we must deal with problems and uncertainty. We can develop the ability to embrace creativity, go beyond the norm, and come up with creative answers to the problems we face. We can find power in our resiliency and come out stronger on the other side, just like the Taj Mahal did when it survived the chaos of war.

CHAPTER 21: ORCHIDELIRIUM

Part 1: The Fact

Something strange occurred in the opulent parlors and well-manicured gardens of Victorian society in the middle of the 19th century.

Wealthy socialites fell victim to a strange addiction known as "Orchidelirium." They were completely obsessed by a curious competition to purchase the most exquisite orchids. These flowers were incredibly trendy, and they created quite a stir in high society.

Part 2: The Story

It all started when rare orchids from far-off regions of the world arrived in England. Orchids were extremely rare, which prompted them to become status symbols, causing quite a passionate frenzy. These exquisite and intricate blooms enthralled the upper class. They took such pride in flaunting their wealth and sophisticated preferences with these flowers.

In search of the most luxurious orchids, gardeners and orchid enthusiasts combed the globe and risked their lives on perilous journeys to distant locales. These brave individuals, known as "orchid hunters," took great risks to bring back rare finds for their peers to admire. Wealthy collectors held intense bidding battles at orchid auctions, pushing the prices to insane heights. The newspapers called them "The Orchid Wars."

The orchid obsession wasn't just about having a nice orchid or two or getting your name in the paper. These high-society people took Orchidelirium a step further and turned their houses into botanical battlegrounds. They built lavish greenhouses inside their mansions so they could display their treasured blossoms.

It wasn't unusual for such orchid collectors to spend a fortune on their prized plants, treating them like fragile, high-maintenance divas by hiring horticultural specialists and paying them extravagant sums of money.

A single orchid bulb could cost more than a home at the height of Orchidelirium. Consider spending a huge amount of money on a single delicate flower that most likely would start wilting the next day. Sure, there are some really beautiful orchids out there, but many of these orchid hunters didn't know how to take care of them on their own to keep them alive. Such was the floral frenzy's lunacy.

This crazy infatuation caused a lot of strange social norms and etiquette in this era. Orchid growers jealously guarded their precious blossoms, frequently refusing to tell anyone about their methods of cultivation or the sources of their rare specimens.

People even hid their orchids away in safe spaces to keep them away from prying eyes and prospective robbers.

Orchidelirium became a sort of secret society with membership restricted to those only with the resources and contacts to acquire these highly sought-after blooms.

Part 3: The Breakdown

Beyond the absurdity, Orchidelirium provides a fascinating window into the psychology of Victorian society. It was a time when the middle class was expanding and trade had a bigger impact. With their exotic origins and high price tags, orchids gave the wealthy a way to set themselves apart from everyone else. The infatuation with these blossoms was a desire to own something rare and unattainable, the ultimate status symbol.

Although we're not as obsessed with orchids as we once were, Orchidelirium is still very much a part of our contemporary culture. Many people still have a strong desire for luxury and exclusivity as they fight to own the newest technology or high-end clothing brands. Orchidelirium serves as a reminder of the persistent human need for status symbols and the extent to which some people would go to acquire them.

The danger of becoming overly concentrated on material things is something that Orchidelirium teaches us as well. It highlights the shallowness of prioritizing status symbols over other, more important areas of life. We should pause and consider the genuine worth of the things we chase in modern society, where consumerism and social media can aggravate this need for validation through tangible possessions. True joy and contentment are rarely found in the brief appeal of things but rather in the deep bonds we create and our shared experiences.

CHAPTER 22:
TO GRANDMA'S HOUSE BY MAIL

Part 1: The Fact

In the beginning years of the United States Postal Service, there weren't exactly very many clear guidelines about what you could or couldn't send in the mail. Different towns got away with different things. It all depended on how their postmaster read the regulations.

As a result, sneaky people started going to their local post offices with all sorts of things to mail like eggs, bricks, snakes, and every other unusual thing you could think of. So naturally, with all this uncertainty, parents took advantage of the new parcel service as a cheap way to send their kids off to grandma's house.

Part 2: The Story

The floodgates opened with unusual package requests as soon as the post office began accepting parcels over four pounds on January 1, 1913. Two of these unusual people were a mother and father who decided to mail their eight-month-old son. They paid 15 cents for his stamps and then handed him over to the mailman, who dropped the baby off at his grandmother's house about a mile away.

There were about six other reports of mailing children over the next two years. It wasn't a common thing to do, but buying stamps for a kid was much cheaper than a train ticket. It just made sense to mail them. Well, not really, but parents weren't too worried about it.

Even though mailing kids seems extremely unrealistic and probably not very safe, it's important to remember that this all took place in a very different time. Early in the 20th century, safety requirements were less strict than they are now. Also, many families knew their local mailman quite well, especially in rural areas. These families weren't just handing their child over to a complete stranger but to a family friend.

In the case of one Idaho six-year-old, her parents handed her over to a postal worker to take her to her grandma's house 73 miles away after paying 53 cents for stamps. The postal worker who took the girl was actually a relative of the family. However, when the postmaster general heard about this super fragile package, he officially banned postal workers from accepting humans as mail.

The new regulations didn't stop some families. After the Idaho incident, one woman mailed her six-year-old daughter from her home in Florida to her father's home in Virginia. That was a whopping 720-mile trip. However, it only cost 15 cents.

It wasn't until a three-year-old made the headlines after being mailed 40 miles to visit her sick mother that the postmasters really began cracking down on sending kids through the mail. People still tried but were unsuccessful. After all, claiming kids to be "harmless live animals" and therefore legal to send through the mail just didn't end up working.

Part 3: The Breakdown

Even though we might gawk at the idea of sending children in the mail, it's important to consider the lessons this bizarre incident can teach us. It reminds us of how far we've come in terms of child welfare and safety. Our children's safety and well-being are top priorities today. To keep people safe, we have strict laws in place. In our modern society, the concept of surrendering our children to a delivery service would be received with total alarm.

This odd historical event emphasizes the value of flexibility and inventiveness. It shows how individuals made inventive use of the resources and services at their disposal to satisfy their needs. Even while the act of mailing children may appear ridiculous to us now, it was a sign of the innovation and out-of-the-box thinking of the time.

Mailing your kids to grandma's house via the postal service may leave us in awe, but it also encourages us to recognize the strides we have achieved in protecting our loved ones. It serves as a reminder of the funny and occasionally odd nature of history as well as the unique ways in which individuals have found solutions to common issues.

CHAPTER 23:
THE FRENCH TOWN THAT WENT MAD

Part 1: The Fact

The picturesque French town of Pont-Saint-Esprit had a bit of a meltdown on one hot summer day in 1951. It was a day that would be remembered as the day the entire town fell into a state of craziness.

Doctors were baffled by the episode, which was later called the "Cursed Bread Incident." Hundreds of people in the town experienced hallucinations and quickly filled the clinics and hospitals.

Part 2: The Story

The story starts out simply enough with the bread delivery at the neighborhood bakery. Nobody thought this ordinary loaf of bread would unravel the entire community. The baker unknowingly bought a loaf of rye bread infested with a fungus.

This particular fungus was known to produce a compound called ergot, which contained alkaloids with hallucinogenic properties. The town was betrayed by delicious bread.

As the unsuspecting townsfolk ate the contaminated bread, they soon began to exhibit many strange symptoms. While some people experienced severe hallucinations, others experienced convulsions, delusions, and a profound sense of hopelessness. The town was transformed into a crazy carnival.

The first victim ran into the local clinic, waving his arms like he was shaking off a horde of bees. Another was convinced snakes were slithering all over his body. The list went on and on. A little girl claimed tigers were chasing her. A postman thought he was shrinking. A woman swore her children were being ground into sausages. A man smashed his furniture to try to rid his house of predators.

Even the animals went crazy. One dog kept biting a stone until its teeth broke. After the first day, around 75 residents had reported seeing hallucinations. Some of the residents later said it was like the apocalypse struck the town.

Where many reportedly saw fantastical creatures skulking in the shadows like dragons or even elusive unicorns prancing through the streets, some had a rather calming experience. Some of the townspeople heard heavenly choruses and saw brilliant flashes of color light up the world in a way they had never seen before. This particular inexplicable experience moved the director of the local farmers' cooperative to write hundreds upon hundreds of pages of poetry.

As the hours passed, the hospitals and asylums in the region quickly filled to capacity. About 300 people ended up complaining of odd sensations like nausea, stomachaches, low blood pressure, weak pulse, insomnia, low body temperature, and cold sweats. The incident lasted several days. Then everything went back to normal. After discovering what caused the madness, they probably had a tough time trusting their bakers.

Part 3: The Breakdown

Even though the Cursed Bread Incident was an isolated incident brought on by contaminated bread, it makes us realize that our decisions and actions have unanticipated results. In today's world, we're constantly exposed to information and influences that might affect our attitudes and actions. Using critical thinking is essential to avoid unintentionally falling for the metaphorical equivalent of contaminated bread.

The incident also highlights how crucial mental health education is. The townspeople's hallucinations and delusions were surely alarming. We must prioritize our mental health and seek help when necessary in the modern environment, where stress and worry are on the rise. The Cursed Bread Incident serves as a sobering reminder that, under the right conditions, the human mind can be both intriguing and delicate.

CHAPTER 24:
HALLEY'S GASES

Part 1: The Fact

Halley's Comet is a celestial visitor that appears in our night sky every 76 years. It's an astrological event that's always piqued our interest. Throughout history, its captivating appearance has sparked both fascination and fear.

In the early decades of the 20th century, this fascinating comet was the subject of many wild speculations about poisonous gases falling to Earth. Several new business endeavors began as a result of this belief, including the intriguing story of the anti-comet pills.

Part 2: The Story

Let's take a moment to absorb the amazing history of Halley's Comet before we dive into the anomalies surrounding this astronomical event. This comet has been studied for countless years and is named after the British astronomer Edmond Halley, who first calculated its orbit. Actually, according to historical documents, its existence has been known as far back as at least 240 BC. Talk about an ancient celeb in the night sky.

Fast forwarding to the early 20th century, technological developments finally made it possible for scientists to witness Halley's Comet up close. These observations produced a startling finding: the comet's tail contained a deadly gas called cyanogen.

The scientific community was in awe at this discovery, but the general public became a little more afraid for their safety. The comet had been safely passing by Earth for centuries, so why these people thought they would suddenly be exposed to dangerous toxins makes no sense.

Con artists decided to take advantage of this news and prey on people's worries. They created a variety of ridiculous items to defend against the "deadly gas" released by Halley's Comet. One of the most famous concoctions was the anti-comet pill. These tablets were promoted as miraculous cures that would protect people from the alleged dangers of the comet's poisonous emissions. These con artists promised safety to those who were taken in by the spell of panic. A pill a day does not keep the comet away.

The pills weren't the only scams out there. People sold gas masks by the gas chamber-load. People stuffed paper around their doorframes to keep the gas out. A really ridiculous invention was the anti-comet umbrella that apparently was supposed to protect you from the approaching comet.

Naturally, the scientific community was quick to expose the silliness of these comet-preventing inventions. Experts and astronomers tried to reassure everyone that any potential danger from cyanogen gas would be completely nonexistent because of the great distance between Earth and

Halley's Comet. Like a whisper lost in a cosmic symphony, the gas would dissolve harmlessly in the void of space.

In the end, Halley's Comet appeared as expected in 1910, and no one ended up in any danger. Unfortunately, there were no refunds, so everyone was stuck with useless pills, umbrellas, and gas masks. The con artists' marketing schemes and dishonest business practices defrauded people from their hard-earned cash. Unfortunately, it appears that human weakness and the need for a quick fix still triumph even in the face of scientific rationality.

Part 3: The Breakdown

The anti-comet pills remind us of how vulnerable people are to fear and false information. We see recurring trends in today's environment that are comparable to how the promise of a magical pill deceived our predecessors. We must be on the lookout for the spread of false information in the age of immediate information and extensive social media.

As we have a tendency to look for simple answers, fear and panic can spread like wildfire. When faced with outrageous statements, it's crucial to use critical thinking, fact-checking, and reliable sources as sources of information.

The anti-comet pill incident emphasizes the value of following experts' advice and the strength of scientific logic. Armed with information and proof, astronomers of the day disproved the erroneous claims made about Halley's Comet without hesitation. We must still put our faith in the rigorous pursuit of truth and scientific inquiry now.

Let Halley's Comet serve as a reminder that wonder, curiosity, and a sense of humor are the best travel companions as we observe the ethereal splendor of Halley's

Comet in the night sky. So, the next time you see a commercial claiming a miraculous cure, think back to the anti-comet medications and laugh at the silliness of it all.

CHAPTER 25: TOMATO ON TRIAL

Part 1: The Fact

Salem, Massachusetts, is known for the Salem Witch Trials in the late 1600s. These trials involved the unnecessary persecution of around 200 people accused of sorcery. This town wasn't the only Salem that held unfair trials.

In 1820, Salem, New Jersey, had its own warped trial that involved a very suspicious figure on the witness stand: an innocent and unsuspecting tomato accused of being a poisonous menace to society.

Part 2: The Story

The story of the tomato's courtroom drama begins in the 1500s when this plump and juicy fruit first entered European homes. As it made its debut, whispers of the fruit's supposedly wicked character started to spread among the more conservative groups. How scandalous could a fruit be?

As the centuries progressed, more and more people began to fear tomatoes. They associated the red color with danger, death, and sin. It was even nicknamed "the poison apple." It didn't help that there were repeated cases of people getting sick or dropping dead after eating tomatoes. What these people didn't realize, especially if they were dead, was that it wasn't the tomatoes poisoning them.

People during this time usually ate on pewter plates. Pewter contains a lot of lead. The highly acidic nature of tomatoes ended up intensifying the levels of lead. In other words, the pewter-lead-tomato combo ended up being the perfect recipe for disaster.

Several more years of distrust passed by, especially because of people like barber and surgeon John Gerard. He believed tomatoes were poisonous due to a toxin called tomatine. Yes, tomatoes do contain tomatine, but in such low amounts that it's hardly harmful. That's why you shouldn't listen to anything your barber tells you unless it has to do with hair. Well, Gerard's beliefs went viral. Everyone thought tomatoes were unfit for human consumption. That was that.

Finally in 1820, Colonel Robert Gibbon Johnson came forward to prove tomatoes weren't poisonous. All rise for the Salem Tomato Trial.

The story goes that Johnson stood outside the Salem courthouse with a basket of tomatoes. After a crowd gathered to watch, he ate every single one. To the amazement of everyone watching, Johnson remained completely conscious, healthy, and free from any symptoms of poisoning. Anyone who came to see a writhing body was surely disappointed. His trial by tomato changed many minds, and the stigma against tomatoes soon vanished.

Part 3: The Breakdown

We frequently make fast decisions and establish

opinions based on inaccurate information or previous assumptions, just as the tomato was misunderstood and unfairly demonized. The tomato trials are a good reminder to keep an open mind while learning new things and to be willing to question the current status quo and our own beliefs.

The tomato's transformation from villain to hero also emphasizes the significance of scientific understanding and knowledge. We became aware of the mistake of our ways as we learned more about the makeup and health advantages of the tomato. This serves as a powerful lesson, reminding us to rely on factual knowledge rather than give in to unfounded tales or stoking fear.

So, keep this odd story in mind the next time you bite into a juicy tomato. Let it serve as a reminder that there are a lot of unusual and amazing things out there just waiting to be discovered and that sometimes all it takes to bring them to their full potential is a little curiosity, a dash of humor, and the willingness to question what we think we know.

AFTERWORD

History is weird, right? Any weird history book is definitely not your typical history book. School might actually be more interesting if our history books were a little weirder. Putting an exciting spin on learning is always a great idea. In the case with this book, we're not only learning about history and how it helped shape our world today, but we're also left with a smile and the thought that the world isn't just weird now.

The weird events that happened in the past remind us there's no such thing as a single human experience. Instead, there have been a lot of unique and odd things that have happened throughout history, each with its own batch of causes and results. By looking at events like the ones described in this book, we can learn more about the long range of human experiences that have existed and still do.

Learning about these crazy events challenges our views and thoughts about what's normal and acceptable in society. Something might have been unimaginable in the past, but the norm now. It proves how society is always changing, and it's not going to stop.

Reading stories like the ones written in this book is a reminder that history is more intricate than a straight line of advancement and enlightenment. Instead, it's a crazy ride with many unforeseen turns. We can better understand the details of the past and the present by accepting the oddity of history.

Finally, it's just plain fun researching weird things. It gives us a chance to explore the unexpected and the often forgotten aspects of our world. There are a ton of odd people and events. Hopefully, you learned about some weird things you didn't quite expect.

We hope you enjoyed *Weird Things in History and Why the Heck They Happened Volume 2*. Together, we traveled through some of the more extraordinary and obscure historical events that maybe made us want to go for a walk and discover what's happening outside right now. Just pretend you're like Huberta the Hippo on a fantastic journey into the unknown! From waves of molasses and snobbish orchid obsessions to town-wide hallucinations and ineffective anti-comet pills, we saw that fact can definitely be stranger than fiction.

We all know there is a lot of weird history out there. Believe it or not, stories like the ones presented here might not even be on a bookshelf or an online article. If you have a past family member who was involved in some kind of super weird historical event or know of something crazy that happened in your community long ago, we'd love to hear about it! When you leave your review of this book, share your weird family history by using *#myweirdhistory* in the review.

Your story could end up in a future installment of *Weird Things in History and Why the Heck They Happened*! Thanks for getting weird with us!

ABOUT THE AUTHOR

Pablo has a passion for history and a knack for humor. Born with an insatiable curiosity, he has spent countless hours diving into the depths of the past, uncovering fascinating stories and forgotten anecdotes.

Pablo's unique talent lies in his ability to blend historical facts with a witty sense of humor, creating entertaining narratives that transport readers to different eras while leaving them with a smile on their faces.

Whether delving into the adventures of ancient civilizations or shedding light on little-known historical events, Pablo's work promises a delightful blend of knowledge and laughter, making history come alive in a way that is both engaging and entertaining.

ENJOY ALL OF MY WRITING PROJECTS

I have a lot of writing projects to share with you. What do they all have in common? Humor! If you like to laugh, I'd love to share my stories with you. The best way to do that is to **subscribe to my Mailing List at https://pablovannucci.com/subscribe**.

FOLLOW ME ON SOCIAL

@VannucciAuthor

COLLECT YOUR WEIRD HISTORY!
Volumes 1, 2 and 3 out now!

THANK YOU FOR LEAVING AN AMAZON REVIEW!

Printed in Great Britain
by Amazon